WITTY NOTES

Pharis Evans, Jr.

WITTY NOTES

WITTY NOTES

Chocolate Chip & Co. Publishing
www.sheridansdavis.com

TABLE OF CONTENTS

WITTY NOTES

DEDICATION

PARENTS
Rev. Pharis D. Evans / Ann N. Evans
BOTHERS
Lester Bernard Evans / Dr. E. Wayne Evans
SISTERS
Rochelle Evans-Howard & Leisa Evans-Broadus
NIECES
Nicole Evans / Aletrice "Woo" Evans / Melody Evans
NEPHEWS
**Shannon L. Evans / DeJuan Watson / Armani Joshua
LeRoy Scott**
PERSONAL FAMILY
Layla / Tyjonn / Velmita

WITTY NOTES

ACKNOWLEDGEMENTS

PASTOR JOSEPH DAVIS
It was YOU, my friend & mentor, who planted a seed in my spirit to share information that's been in a holding cell inside of me. It was your constant belief, encouragement, and push as to how this book came to fruition...
Thank you buddy ☺

GINA M. WRIGHT
It was YOU who opened my mind to broader aspects in many facets of life...from music to writings.
It was on YOUR coffee table that I found inspiration that would finally reveal the progressive revelation for
"Witty Notes."

WITTY NOTES

My Children:
LAYLA Shanice Evans *and* **TYJONN Donyell Lockett**
I hope that these documented proverbs will become watered
seeds within your thought process...
helping you grow from being great, mannerable children to
mature, classy, respectable & wise adults.

LIFE
Without the Day-To-Day Circumstances You've Allowed Me to
Experience Personally, and From A Far...
... I'd Have No Witt To Note.

THANKS

PERSONAL LONG-TIME LOVED ONES

Rod / Tuff / Angie / Fats / Carl / Cynt J. / P. Porter / D. Carr
Hubb / Nicole / DeJuan / Mat / Vel / Davie / Christine
Love connections never remain unbroken…. in fact by the time
this very book is PRINTED and PUBLISHED, any one of our
connections may become disconnected. However, I will never
overlook or disregard the
longtime "Love-Support", Fellowship, Followship, and
Friendship that each of you have PRINTED in my heart, and
PUBLISHED in my life. In way or another you all have held me
up - no matter the sacrifice…
no matter the disagreements … no matter me being me…

you guys loved, gave, and made PEJ happen. I unselfishly and without pride thank and acknowledge each of you.
(*noted: Monday, July 16, 2018 – 1:49 A.M.*)

THE EDITORS Of ANY Of MY PRINT
Tonya C. / Donna B-B./ Gina W. / Nicole E.
Devlon P. / Leisa E-B. / Vanessa R.
Over the years (1998-2019) - it's because of you my most important documented words make readable sense.
I appreciate your Time, Eyes, Mind, and most of all your Heart to help me with the TLC you do.

"Thanx Real Much" – "Much Real Love"

PROCLAMATIONS

"**Witty Notes**" can be considered one of the most unique conversational coffee books written and discussed. Although author Pharis Evans Jr. is a licensed and ordained Minister (now Pastor), yet he still remains to have a witty outlook on life. His reality is life's truth - not every conversation is ministry based. Not every conversation around the water cooler, dinner table, or various socials is about "God"

...and no disrespect to God at all, because even in the word of God (Proverbs 8:12) it states, "*I wisdom dwell with prudence, and find out knowledge*

WITTY NOTES

*of **WITTY** inventions.*" Thus this book is one of Witty written inventions that offers the mind a different point to take, make, and debate ...lol. There's simply nothing wrong with interesting, thought provoking, fun nuggets to chew on and share... just remember they are only "Personalized Proverbs" by Pharis Evans Jr. that you just might agree with and enjoy.

FOREWORDS

REV. CLAY EVANS/UNCLE CLAY

I want you to know that as your uncle, I am very proud of you and all of your accomplishments. Your daddy, myself along with your other uncles and aunts have done much to build the "Evans" name to be what it is. And I'm believing in you (Phario) to take this legacy further. Uncle loves you and may the Lord bless you real, real good.

WITTY NOTES

SAMUEL R. BLAKES

One of the greatest benefits to my life has been the many principles of wisdom that have been imparted to me through simple conversations. Proverbs 15:25 talks about the power of the right words spoken at the right time. In this book, Pharis Evans, Jr. shares with us some small principles, that if applied will make big impacts on our lives. I challenge you to look introspectively as you read these writings, and I promise that you will find principles that will not only excite you but also ignite you for next level living.

WITTY NOTES

NUGGETS

WITTY NOTES

**No One Can Validate Your Greatness
Like Your Character & Heart Can.**
Allow Your Character To Be
Your Spokesman.

Tell Positive Truth

Faith Doesn't Have A Thought Process; It Has A Belief System.

Faith Doesn't Think...It Believes

WITTY NOTES

**Quoting The Bible With Our Actions
Is Far More Upright Than
Quoting It With Our Mouths.**

Humbly Live Righteous

WITTY NOTES

Stay Clear Of Negativity...
It'll Have A Positive Effect On Your Life.

**Extending Kindness Despite
Offense and Harm,
May Award Favor and Grace
Despite Justice.**

Do Good Despite Bad Done

People Who Don't Want To Give You Credit
Will One Day Read Your Name In Credits.

Ignoring Doesn't Mean It's Not There

WITTY NOTES

**The Best Advantage To
Sitting On The Bench:
You Have a Front Row Seat To
Learn What's Going On In The Game.**

WITTY NOTES

Patience Begins The Moment You Start Waiting.

It's Easy To Count On The Ones
Who Didn't Count You Out.

Don't Add Where You Should Subtract

WITTY NOTES

It's Not Safe To Make Decisions While
You Are Heated...
The Right One Just Might Get Burned Up.

A Relaxed Mind Makes Kool Results

WITTY NOTES

**You Don't Have To Comply
To The Industry's Rules
If You've Succeeded In Victories
By Way Of Your Own Playbook.**

Do What Works For You

WITTY NOTES

**Change Is Inevitable
Unless One's Destination Is
Where & How They Are.**

Remove From Remaining

WITTY NOTES

We Often Have To <u>Take</u> People
For Who They Are,
But Most Times Have To <u>Leave</u> Them
Where They're Determined To Be.

Don't Waste Miles On The Helpless & Hopeless

WITTY NOTES

I Would Rather Own
100% Of My Little Bit
Than To Own
A Little Bit Of My 100%

You Get What You Negotiate

Quitting Actually IS An Option,
It's Just Not The Right Choice.

Not Every Option is Worth Considering

WITTY NOTES

**Pride Is That One Disease
That Can and should be lost
Before It Finds A Home In Your Spirit.**

Your Character & Relationships Deserve To Live

**Being Grown Enough To Drink
Doesn't Mean Mature Enough
Not To Get Drunk
Either Way, Don't Drink & Drive!!!**

Be Mature No Matter What Age

It's Hard To Believe
Verbal Answers Without Results.
Although It May Be True...
Having Proof Speaks Without Words.

Walk The Talk

WITTY NOTES

If You Just Must Give Up,
Never Give Up On Yourself.

There's A Work In You That Must Be Done

**If We Continue To Give People
What They Haven't Tried To Earn,
They May Never Work For It!**

Work Equals Earned

WITTY NOTES

If We Continue To Give People What They Don't Deserve, They May Never Appreciate It!

Appreciate What's Deserved

WITTY NOTES

Musicians & Athletes:
**Not All Results Are Impressive,
Much That May Be Impressive Doesn't
Always Produce The Best Results.**

Play The Right Way

WITTY NOTES

**LQQKing For Certain People
To Do and Be Certain Things
@ Certain Times
Is Like Playing Hide & Seek With A Ghost.**

You Can Never Find What Not Seeable

**Awards
Are the Results of Dues Paid...
Rewards
Are the Results of Deeds Done.**

Earn Your Results

WITTY NOTES

If More Time Is Spent On
BEING Right...
Than DOING Right
Everything Will Fall Right In Place.

Prioritize BEING Over DOING

**Experiencing Pro-bono Grace Means
Everything You Got Cost Less
Than You Paid... Thus
It Doesn't Cost To Say "Thank You."**

Appreciation Is A Down Payment On Future Favor

WITTY NOTES

Many Days It's Hard To Breathe.
Due To **Living** a Life
Filled with **Dead**lines.

Give Yourself More Room To Breathe

WITTY NOTES

No Matter The Name of a Condition,
Everyone Is Normal...
Some of Us Just Have Special Needs.

Normal People With Different Needs

WITTY NOTES

**Loosing Loved Ones In Life
Sometimes Hurts More
Than Loosing Loved Ones To Death.**

Cherish Loved Ones

WITTY NOTES

I Never Changed My Love For
Some People...
They Just Changed How I Show It.

Wise & Safe Love In Affect

WITTY NOTES

People Who Are Negative Minded
By Seeing The Worst In Life,
Are Absolutely Positively
Mentally & Spiritually Blind.

See The Positive

Being Fair With Everybody
Does Not Mean
You Treat Everybody The Same.

Love Varies

It's "Favor Damaging" For People
To Have Made It To Where They Are
But Seemingly Forget
How They Got There.

Burnt Bridges Can't Be Traveled

WITTY NOTES

When One Learns How To
Work With Their Limitations...
They Will Not Over Exaggerate
Their Options.

No Need To Supersede The Necessary

WITTY NOTES

Music Is More Than Just Sonic Sound It's Audio Art.

Visualize The Sound

WITTY NOTES

**Those Who Deal With You
By Way Of Their Convenience
Do Not Deserve Your Sacrifice.**

Sacrificial Worthiness Is In Order

WITTY NOTES

Sometimes God Has to Strip You to Redress You.

WITTY NOTES

When You Meet A Person Who Turns
Out To Be Different Than You Met,
The Fact Remains
That You Know A Stranger.

Time Will Reveal Truth

Tragedies Reveals Truths About the Reality Of People, Places & Things.

Believe the Revelation

An Assumption Is the Riskiest Understanding One Can Have.

Clarity & Closure Is Most Safe

WITTY NOTES

Don't Make It A Habit Of Lowering Your Standards Due to Another's Acceptance.

Everything Accepted May Not Be Best to Offer

Don't Hold Your Heart Captive When One Has Freed Their Mind From Your Feelings.

Decrease the Sentencing Time of Hurt

WITTY NOTES

Because I Know How Bad I Am…
Yet See How Blessed I Am…
Serves as Daily Proof of How Good
GOD IS.

That's Despite of Me Love

**Conversing with The Illogical
By Using Logic
Is Like Trying to Reason With
The Unreasonable.**

One Can't Apprehend What They Can't Comprehend

Pro Bono Can't Afford
A Deadline to Be Meant.

There's No Demands on Grace

From Whom You Find False Humility,
Is from Whence False Compliments
Come From.

Don't get Caught Up

WITTY NOTES

**No Matter How Much Talent One Has
...It Could Very Well Be A Detriment
If the Talent Is Not Used Humbly.**

You Can Miss Reaching A Heart
By Aiming At Impressing The Mind

Rosa Parks Stood When She Sat.
Standing Does Not Always
Depend On Legs and Feet...
But Courage and Character.

Stand for Something That's Easy To Sit Down On

WITTY NOTES

Knowing Jesus
Equals A Happy Ending!

Heaven Bound Results

You Can Never Tell Anyone Anything Who Knows Everything.

Don't Speak in Vain

WITTY NOTES

When Hype Dies Down...
We're Left with A Life of Reality.

Most Times It Is What It Ain't

There's Really Only One
True Side to A Story –
Anything Else That's Considered A Side
...Is Not the Story...It's A Tail.

It Only Is What It Only Is

Sometimes One's Truest <u>Value</u> Depends on The <u>Worth</u> to Another.

Consider the Worth to Understand the Value

**Many Friends to The Famous
May Really Be Respecters of Persons.
When the Fame Is Gone...
So Goes the Respect.**

There's A Difference in Knowing What One Is & Who One Is

WITTY NOTES

**Denominations Causes Separation
Due to Interpretation
Which Results to Division.**

There Are More Sets of Churches Than Gangs
... Who's Really At War?

If You've Got the One and Only God
(The Creator of the World)
You've Got It Plenty Good
Without HIM…You're Doomed.

No GOD… No Good

WITTY NOTES

**Why Express Yourself
If It Gets Disregarded?
Save Your Words & Spare Your Feelings.**

Sincerity Is Too Valuable to Be Ignored

**The Reason Things Won't
Change** (for the better) **For Certain People
Is Because Certain People Won't Change**
...for the better.

A Change Brings About A Change

WITTY NOTES

**Don't Allow Your Allegiance
To Certain Ones
Block A Relationship
With Other Ones.**

Let No One Interrupt What's meant To Be Connected

WITTY NOTES

Re: Gossip:
Sometimes What One Chooses to Know Does Not Mean It's True to Know.

Confirm the Knowledge

WITTY NOTES

**You Can Only Count On
Those Who Are Not Accountable
...To Not Be Counted On.**

Accountability Doesn't Miscount

WITTY NOTES

Those with A Low % Of Authenticity Have Not Completely Found Themselves.

Originality Is One of a Kind

WITTY NOTES

Don't Overly Concern Yourself With Copycats - They May Copy the Items On Your Menu, But Don't Know The Ingredients In Your Recipe.

No One Can Do You Better Than You

WITTY NOTES

Re: Relationship
There's A Difference Between HEARING What One Says... And UNDERSTANING Why It's Said!

Listen with The Intent to Understand

Re: Relationship
**If You Have Not Sacrificed,
Please Don't Mention What All You've
Conveniently Done & Gave!**

Use Humble & Fair Wisdom

**One's True Unconditional Love Will
Show Even When Another's Love
Hasn't Been Felt
Due to Unloving Conditions.**

Let Love Be Showered from Many Faucets

**People Don't Have to Be
In Your Face to Be IN Your Life…
& Some People That Are in Your Face
May Not Be Best FOR Your Life.**

Face the Truth

Don't Allow the Memory of Hurt to Harbor the Effect of Hurt.

Be Free from Past Hurt.

Let Hurt Leave

WITTY NOTES

People Who Are Not Accountable
Have A Very Estranged
Relationship with The Truth.

Don't Lie to Reality

Those Who Are Convicted Due to Wrong,
Are Truly Sorry for Their Actions...
Who Are Those Who Are Remorseful...?
Who Are Those Who Apologize...?
Who Are Those Who Make A Change?

Feelings Invoke Words That Provoke Change

**Everybody That's Good TO You
Isn't Necessary Good FOR You.**

Principals Over Pleasures

There's A Qualified Difference In
How Long One Has Done Something
And How Good They Are At It.

Time Does Not Determine Talent

WITTY NOTES

One Does Not Have To Have A Degree In Order To Be Educated.

WITTY NOTES

**All Seasons Come To An End...
Thus We Must
Mentally, Emotionally and Spiritually
Dress Accordingly.**

Understand The Forecast

WITTY NOTES

Some People, Places & Things In Life Are
Best Described As
A Beautiful Disaster.

WITTY NOTES

Understanding What Not to Expect Can Prevent Disappointment.

Thus, Change Your Expectation.

Expect & Accept The Reality

**Just Because Someone Isn't
Where You Are When You Are There
Doesn't Mean They've Never Been.**

One's Present Doesn't Determines One's Past

Being Liked Doesn't Gain One Respect,
It May Just Gain One Company.
But What Good Is Company
That's Not Respecting of Another.

Not All Respected Are Liked

WITTY NOTES

There's So Much You May Not Know,
But What You Do Know Is
Unmistakable Knowledge.

It Would Be A Mistake to Fake What You Don't Know

Music & I Relate
Without Me Having To Speak...

It Speaks To & For Me.

One Person Dialog

It's Impossible To Be Positive Without Faith.

A Mountain Can't Be Moved By Thought
... It's Moved By Belief

An Attitude Of Faith:
Visual Proof Is Not Needed
If The Giver Is Failure Proof.

God Never Fails... He Himself Is Proven

WITTY NOTES

**Achieve Belief
Before You Receive
So You Can Receive What You Believed.**

Water Your Faith Seeds With Belief

The Chicago Cubs' Manager Joe Maddon
Got His First Major League Job
at The Age of 51... and
Won His First World Series in 2016
...at the Age of 63

Age Ain't Nothin' But A Number That Shows You're Still Around
#It'sNeverTooLate

Some People Can Never Be Helped For Wanting to Always Be Right.

You Can't Help The Helpless & Hopeless

**Your Talent Can Get You There
But Your CHARACTER
Can Take You Even Further.**

BEING Good Is better Than DOING Good

WITTY NOTES

**Don't Allow Negative Thinking
To Cancel Your Faith.**

Negative Thinkers Lack Faith

WITTY NOTES

It's Better to Prevent the Problem
(beforehand)
Then Try to Fix A Problem
(afterwards)
Try Starting with The Cause.

Much Pre-Production Help Save Post-Production

**It's Most Difficult for Pride to Speak
The Fewest Of Words...**
I'm Sorry / I'm Wrong / My Fault
I Apologize / You're Right / My Mistake

It Takes Less Than One Second
To Say Two Words That Can Live For Lifetime

**True Humility
Never Has To Point Itself Out...
It's Easily Recognizable**

Quiet Impacts Are Felt, Not Heard

WITTY NOTES

**Negative Thinking
Is A Detour Away From
Positive Knowledge.**

WITTY NOTES

A Nasty Attitude
Is Like A Bounced Check...
It Can Leave A Mark on Your Account,
& Others Won't Trust to Deal.

Don't Deplete Relationships

**Positive Testimonies
Should Not End on A Negative
Note or Highlight.**

Don't Erase The Goodness That Gave Reason To Testify In The First Place

WITTY NOTES

Hype Without Results
Is The Truest Fake News.

...Trump That

It's Just Not What It's Not

One Who Normally Has A Problem
With Everybody
Is More Than Likely The Problem
Themselves.

Self-Evaluation Is Rare But Needed

WITTY NOTES

It's Most Best To
Listen With Intent To Understand.

**No One Is Entitled To Anything
Outside Of An Understood Earning…
Thus, If It's Received…
Count It As Grace.**

Grace, Is Un-Earned Favor That Has No Merit

WITTY NOTES

Paying Tithes Is Like Giving Little For Much.

Keeping 90% Getting Back another 100%
...and the process repeats itself over & over

One of The Biggest Waste Is
Sharing Wisdom with Someone Who
Does Not Value Wise Counsel
via Transparent Experience.

Info Devalued Is Of No Help To The Ignorant

A Mentor Is Not One Who's Older,
It's One Who's Learned the Right Moves
Due to Them Making Wrong Moves...
But Is A Winner.

Experienced Ones Make The Best Teachers

When It Comes To Growing...
The One Thing We Should Never
Began Doing Is > Quitting.

Don't Give Up On Starting

There's A Vast Difference In
One Showing Respect
&
One Actually Respecting.

Both Deserved – One Earned

It's Impossible For People With NO Remorse To Truly Be Sorry.

Inward Feeling Have Outward Proof

WITTY NOTES

**Most Fronts
Differ Behind The Back.**

When Actions Differ From Words

**Loudly Saying Amen
When the Preacher Is Preaching
Does Not Mean One Is NOT Guilty
Regarding What's Being Preached.**

Smoky Church Mirrors

You Can't Always Embrace the Privilege Without Enduring the Problem.

Can't Have Unearned Rights.

Many Years of Struggles Deserves More Than One Month of Celebration
B H M

The Very Thing People Don't Want
You To Think About Them
Is The Very Thing
They Struggle With Not Being.

True Being Controls All Thoughts

**People Who Are Impressed With
The Wrong Thing
Most Often Aspire That Thing...
But for The Wrong Reason.**

Impressing Without Purpose Is Self-Flattery

Not Everyone Who Commits the Crime Will Feel the Guilt... Thus, Don't Expect an Apology.

However, Victims Must Not Be **Guilty** of None Forgiveness.

Forgiveness Is Righteous

WITTY NOTES

Being Kind to People Who's Been Unkind to You Takes Nothing Away from You But Pride.

**God Is Making Some Of Us
Take the Scenic Route
To the Next Rest Station.**

There's A Purpose For The Path

WITTY NOTES

**Because HE Went to The Cross...
we Don't Have To Go To Hell.**

Denomination Doesn't Save... Jesus Does

128 | p e j

No Matter How Awesome
The Vocal Riff My Be,
No Matter the Chops Played by The Band,
If You Don't Have A SONG...
None of It Really Matters :-/

Musical Priorities

God Often Supplies the Need Before He Reveals There Is A Need. Thus, We Have Unexpected Supply From An Expected Supplier.

God Coverage

WITTY NOTES

Not All Blessings Service Desires...

The Greater Ones Service Needs.

God Prioritizes Needs Over Desires

WITTY NOTES

The Thing About Giving Up:
It Doesn't Get You Anywhere...
It Just Keeps You Where You've Been.

**Being Happy With What's Good To You
Can Never Take the Place Of
Being Fulfilled With
What's Good for You.**

Decide on What Best & Purposed For Your Life

WITTY NOTES

As It Relates to Problems & Issues...
If You've Gone Through It
There's No Need to Hold on To It
Once It's Over.

WITTY NOTES

You Never Really Know Who's in Your
Corner Until You Are in The Corner...
...& They Are There Helping
Pull U Out of The Corner.

Not Everyone Will Leave Your Back Against The Wall

WITTY NOTES

I Believe That Which Is
Constantly Proven...
And GOD Has Proven
HE Is Constantly Good

Proof Is Truth

**Doing What's Easy Doesn't Equate To
Doing What's Right (or best) ...
The Right Choice Is The Best Choice.**

Choose Wisely

The Thing That Makes Anyone A Professional at What They Do Is the Proper MINDSET.

What's In (or not in) The Mind Determines The Actions

WITTY NOTES

**No Matter How Bad Times Are,
It Doesn't Change How Good God Is.**

Reality Is Always True

WITTY NOTES

Man's Election
Can Never Override
God's Selection!!!

The Revelation Of Delegation

WITTY NOTES

One Can Not Deeply Appreciate Success
Without Witnessing
Failures & Struggles.

Appreciate What's Hard to Have

WITTY NOTES

**Some People Are Mislead
Because They Aren't Easily Led.**

Everyone Needs A Leader/Mentor.

WITTY NOTES

Wisdom Is Only An Opinion
Until It's Proven.

One Can't Know It All If One Has Done Nothing

WITTY NOTES

Humbled Greatness Doesn't Have To Strive To Sound Off & Stand Out, It Can Sit Back While Many Find It Out & Point It Out.

WITTY NOTES

One Being Good at Something Is Not
Based On Them Being Good At Doing
That Something...It's Based On
Them Being Good at Knowing It.

The Best Coaches Were Not the Best Players

**Even On Your Healthiest Day
You Are Sick Enough To Die.**

Thank God For New Mercies Daily

WITTY NOTES

**Complaining About What We
DON'T Have...
Is An Insult To The Grace Of God.**

**Sooner Or Later Wisdom Teaches:
You Should Only Give As Much
As One Can Appreciate.**

Be Wise & Don't Waste

WITTY NOTES

If One Isn't Useful to God...

They Are Useless in Life.

Be Useful & Not Useless

**Guarantee Continued Success
By Making Your Ceiling
Your New Floor.**

Reach Above Your Beneath

To Be Accepted By Someone
(or into something)
That's Not Embracing...
Is Not really True Acceptance.

A Meaning Of Inside Out

One Will Never Get Use To Being Accepted Until They Get Over Their Fear Of Being Rejected.

Sometimes We Can Be Our Own Roadblock

**Because the Shoe Fit
Doesn't Mean the Message
Was Designed with You In Mind.**
However, Have A Mind to Walk Better.

Get Your Paranoia Under Control

It's Draining When One Shares Their
Problems with You...
But Not Open to Receiving A
Resolve from You.

Not Being Open Minded Keeps Emotions Caged In

In Extending Grace and
Showing Kindness By Doing Deeds,
It May Be Best Not To
Expect A Return of Appreciation.

Be Pleased with One's Self By Pleasing Others

Forcing Good Deeds On Someone When They Didn't Ask For It... More Than Likely They Will Not Value It...No Matter How Good.

Don't Diminish Your Own Deeds

**Some People Look To Blame Others
For Their Outcome
Because They Are Not Accountable
For Their Input.**

Own Your Own

**Treat People Better
Than They Treat You...
And God's Grace Will
Treat You Best.**

Day To Day Trick Or Treat

WITTY NOTES

We Can Not Have A New Attitude With Old Behavior.

A Renewed Will Change Old Ways

Those Who Listen With Their Heart,
Receives Passion As > Love.
Those Who Listen With Their Feelings,
Confuses Passion With > Attack.

One Never Has To Defend Themselves From Love.... Not Even Tough Love

WITTY NOTES

If The Decisions We Make In Life Hinders The Purpose In Our Future, We've Made Some Wrong Choices.

Wisdom Over Emotion

WITTY NOTES

Changing Wrong Ways Is The Solution To Getting Righteous Results.

There's No Right Way To Do Wrong

WITTY NOTES

As A Visionary:
The Thing Sleep Does Most
Is Allow Me To Dreams
About My Future.

My Mind Never Sleeps

**A Man Knows Himself Best
When He Spends Time Alone...
Alone With Only Him and His Truths.**

Aloneness Invokes Awareness

WITTY NOTES

One Cashing Loyalty In For Opportunity,
Makes Them A Disloyal Opportunist.

Take Advantage Of The Opportunity To Be Loyal

ANTIDOTES

WITTY NOTES

You Can't Share Certain Things
With Certain People
Because Certain People Can't Handle
Knowing Certain Things... *& That's For Certain*

Everything Is not For Everybody

There May Be People In Your Life
Who You Never Imagined Would
Abandon You... Not Knowing
Them Leaving Would Spare Your Life.

Dependent Tears Un-wiped Are Cried In Vain

WITTY NOTES

Respecting One For Their Character
More Than Their Title,
Makes Your Respect Worth Having.

WITTY NOTES

Allow No One To Get The Best OF You By Bringing The Worst OUT of You.

Give No One The Benefit Of The Doubt Who Already Positively Let You Down Time After Time ☹

Trust Them To Fail You

WITTY NOTES

Re: Your Gift:
**Never Let What You Don't Have In Life
Stop You From Sharing
All You Have To Offer Up.**

WITTY NOTES

You May Not Have Much...
But
Use What You Have.

God Will Bless Your Vision With Provision

**Genuine Relationships
Are Worth The Connection
Thus
No Need To Pretend
To Water Fake Plants.**

Be True

Don't Let Your Circumstance
(good or bad)
Change Your Character.

Good Principals, Morals & Standards
Will Forever Be Respected

WITTY NOTES

Don't Waste Time
Giving Respectful Attention
To Someone With Disrespectful Words.

Not Every Insult Requires A Response

Understand:
A Valley Can Only Exist Because Of
2 Or More Mountains...
Keep Moving & Keep Climbing.

Mountain Top Bound

People Who Do What They Do
Because Of You Doing It,
Yet Try To Out Do You, Are Impressed
With How You Do What You Do,
& Wish They Could Do As You Do.

Trail Blazers Never Follow Trails.... They Blasé Them

WITTY NOTES

**Being Alone Doesn't Mean
You Have To Be Lonely.**
*Learn To Love On You...
It's Cheaper & Safer.*

You Are Most Compatible With Yourself

When Things Go Bad...
Don't Forget How The Good Looked –
So You Can Recognize & Appreciate It
When It Comes Back Around.

Due To God's Grace... Bad Is Only Temporary

**When Defeat Assumes
You Are Down For The Count
Grace Will Stand You Up
&Then Victory Shows Up.**

The Fight is Fixed

WITTY NOTES

**Do Not Allow Disbelievers
To Cause U To Discontinue.**

Believe & Forward March

WITTY NOTES

**2 Words
For Any Who May Be
Down, Discouraged or Despondent**
1.) **SMILE** 2.) **AWAY**

Smiling Reveals A Happy Face

The 2 Things That's Gotten Us All From Day To Day Has Been GRACE & MERCY.

Without Grace & Mercy Life Would Be Hard To Live

WITTY NOTES

**Whenever It Seems Madness
Is Taking Place In Your Life,
Just Know God's Promises
Will Make Their Presence Known.**

Hold On...& God Will Hold Off

If OTHERS **Only Knew What Some Of Us Have To Go Though To Provide The Results** THEY **Desire, It Would Be A More Worth While Relationship.**

Appreciate The Sacrifice Before The Gift

WITTY NOTES

Right Behind The Trial That You Are
Currently Facing Is Your Breakthrough.
Just Keep Holding On...
The Fight Is Fixed!

Behind The Scenes Awaits Your Victory

WITTY NOTES

**When You Look Around & Realize
Who's No Longer By Your Side…
It Makes It Easier To See**
that **God** *STILL* **Is**

By Your Side He Will Always Be

**Whatever Decisions We Make,
We Must Live With Them.
Whatever Deals We Break,
We Must Deal With Them.**

Think Before Action

WITTY NOTES

Taking Something, Or Someone
For Granted Reveals The Worth Value
When It, Or They
Are No Longer Available.

Appreciate That Which You've Been Blessed To Have
While You Have It.

WITTY NOTES

**Do For People The Things
You Wished People Had Done For You
...But Didn't.**

...and then watch your harvest grow.

Give What Wasn't Given
#UnconditionalGiver

Integrity Is The Most Respected Gene In The Bloodline Of Character.

Being Integral Invokes Respect & Trust

As A Music Producer:
In Editing, I Look For What's Wrong.
In Mixing, I Listen For What's Wrong.
But In Life, I Look & Listen For My Wrong.

The Mirror Never Lies

WITTY NOTES

**Don't Allow Your Misunderstanding
To Mislead You To The Point
Where You Miss Out On The Point.**

Confirmation Is A Must

Re: *BREAKING BAD HABITS*
It's Not Really A Challenge...
If There Is No Effort.

Put Forth An Effort In Order To Accomplish Goal

**Appraising One's Heart
Can Give Better Understanding
To The Value Of Their Intent.**

Intents Explains Actions

WITTY NOTES

When One's Motive Is Full Of Vanity Their Results Are An Empty Victory

Righteous Doing Awards Righteous Results

Re: Rendering Before People
**Being Nervous
Is A Form of Humility.**
Thus Let Go and Let God.

Depend On Self Less...& Depend On God Most

WITTY NOTES

Because An Opinion Is Asked Does Not Mean An Answer Was NOT Already In Mind.

Humbled Responses Are More Respected

WITTY NOTES

**Concern Yourself Less With
People, Places &Things
You Can't Help.**

Be Free From Stress

WITTY NOTES

**Not Everyone With You
Is Happy For You...
However
Harden Not Your Heart.**

Love Regardless

WITTY NOTES

Everyone That You've Laid It All Out For
May Not Often Lift A Finger For You
In Times Of Need…
But Harden Not Your Heart…LOVE.

Good Is Returned To Good

WITTY NOTES

Not Everyone You Sacrifice For Will Lift A Finger For You.

Love Wisely and Aware

WITTY NOTES

Sometimes Those CLOSEST To You Can Push You The FURTHEST Away.

Loving Certain People Can Be Hazardous For Your Health...so Love With Caution

...but love.

Don't Allow Your Heart To Be A Hazardous To Your Love

WITTY NOTES

**Staring Into Your Past
Prevents Change
From Making An Appearance
In Your Future.**

WITTY NOTES

**You Can't Run Away From Yourself
The Real You Will Always
Make An Appearance.**

Face The You That needs To Be Faced

Value Communication with Those
Who Will Hear with Their Heart,
Take Heed & Regard the Sincere Cries
...If Not...The Wolves Win.

Dependent Tears Un-wiped Are Cried In Vain

**Those That Help You
In Your Bondage,
Are Those You Must Bless
In Your Promise Land.**

**Never Be Surprised by What
A Loved One Might Do to You,
Not Everything Comes From
A Place of Love** ☹

Loved Ones Can Do and Say the Unlinked

If Anyone in Your Life
Is Not Adding to Your Life ...&
Won't Allow You to Add To Their Life
... It's A Subtraction Of Life ☹

Do The Math of Logic

WITTY NOTES

Much In Life Is A Choice...
Thus I Encourage You To Choose To
Be Mentally Healthy...Other Choices May
Be Hazardous for Living ☐

Choose A Life Worth Living

Nothing Or No One Can Keep You Down When God Raises You Up.

God Is the Greatest Lift You Can Get

WITTY NOTES

**Certain People Don't Wanna
Fool WITH You
If They Can't Make A
Fool OUT OF You.**

Be No One's Fool

No One Can Defame the Goodness of Your Character If Good Results Of Character Precedes You.

Proven Characteristics Speaks Loudest

WITTY NOTES

**There's No Such Things As
The Odds Being Against You
When God Is (even) With You.**

God Beats All Odds

Sincere Remorse Leads To True Change

No True Remorse...No True Change.
No True Change Because No True Remorse.

Conviction Invokes Apology
Remorse Invokes > Change

One Doesn't Have to Justify
What's Proven.

People Do What/Who/When/Where & How They Want

Apologies Without A Strive for Change Is Unrealistic Remorse.

WITTY NOTES

**Don't Chase the Things
You're Never Gonna Get,
Because You Didn't Embrace The Things
You Are Supposed To Have.**

Prioritize God's Agenda For Your Life...& All Else Shall Be Added

Another Should Not Be Granted
The Control for Who Loves You.
The Heart of One Can Not Be
Confirmed by The Mind Of Another.

True Love Is Confirmed By Life's Test Of Opportunity.

WITTY NOTES

**Don't LQQK For Someone to Show Up
(for you)
Whose GPS Is Powered by Emotions…
They Will Get Lost in Their Feelings.**

Only Expect What's Proven

WITTY NOTES

A Lapse of Time Does Not Fix Problems.
One Has to Repair What's Broken.
No Matter How Long It Takes.

Be Responsible To Be Accountable

WITTY NOTES

If You Are Set Apart ...Those In Your Life
That's A Part Of Your Set...
Must Respect Your Assigned Purpose.

You Are Accountable For The Purpose Of Your Assignment

No One Is Accountable For Your
Assignment But You.
You Are Held Responsibility...
They Have Nothing To Lose.

Don't Let Another's Lack Be Your Lost

WITTY NOTES

Don't Be Talented Enough To Someone Else, But Not Gifted Enough to Be Your (Own) Self.

Identify You...Own You & Be You

WITTY NOTES

I'd Rather Be Among One Who Does Not Value Me Because They Don't Know My Worth – Than to Be with Any Who Knows My Worth, But Don't Value, Or Appreciate Me.

Identify You...Own You & Be Be You

WITTY NOTES

Never Give One Who's Immature
The Power to Downsize You.

Keep Your Class Super-Sized

WITTY NOTES

Re: The Artistry…
Doing More Does Not Mean…
Doing Better

Over Doing Is Under Achieving

**It's Hard to Make People A Priority
When They've Made You An Option.**

"Love" Should Not Be Convenient ...It Should Be Embraced

WITTY NOTES

PERSONAL PRESCRIPTIONS

HONORABLE MENTIONS

WITTY NOTES

"Never Let Anyone's Badness Determine
How Less Good You Should Be...
Love Regardless."

- Rev. Pharis D. Evans
Pastor/Daddy

WITTY NOTES

"Never Let Anyone Spit In For Face And Tell You It's Raining."

A Rule Of Thumb For Being Intelligent

- Ann N. Evans 1977
Momma (RIP)

WITTY NOTES

"Make New Mistakes, 'son'."

- Lester Bernard Evans 1984
Oldest Brother & Mentor (RIP)

"Observation Is The First Key Of Knowledge."

- **Lester Bernard Evans** 1988
Oldest Brother & Mentor (RIP)

WITTY NOTES

Re: Artistry & Production:
**"Always Be YOU
In The Current Day and Time."**

WITTY NOTES

"Expectation Without Understanding
Can Lead To Disappointment."

-Bishop T.D. Jakes 1996
Employer & Acting Pastor

WITTY NOTES

"The Soprano Part Is The Top Part...
Not The High Part – Anybody Can Reach
Anything If It's In Their Range"

- Dr. Erral Wayne Evans 2001
Older Brother

WITTY NOTES

Re: Presentations:
*"Nephew***...Aim For The Masses,
Not The Classes."**

- **Rev./Dr. Clay Evans** 2002
Uncle, Iconic Pastor, & Mentor

WITTY NOTES

"Forgiveness
Does Not Require
Fellowship."

- **DJ Rogers** 2002
Business Manager, Artist & Mentor

WITTY NOTES

"It's Not An Opinion If It's The Truth."

- **Rev./Dr. Clay Evans** 2003
Uncle, Iconic Pastor, & Mentor

"I Pastor One Church...
But I'm Not Everyone's Pastor.
Some Will Not Let You Pastor Them,
So Do What You Can For Who You Can."

- **Rev. Pharis D. Evans** 2004
Pastor/Daddy

WITTY NOTES

Re: Studying & Preaching:
"What The Words Say...
And What The Words Mean...
Are Two Different Things.
You gotta preach what it means"

- **Pastor Terry Wayne Brooks** 2004
Personal Brother

WITTY NOTES

Re: Being A Public Figure
"Phario...**People Are Your Commodity."**

- **Rev./Dr. Clay Evans** 2005
Iconic Pastor, Uncle, & Mentor

WITTY NOTES

"If You Spend Time Arguing With A Fool...
Who's Really The Fool? ... *now!*"

- **Maulty C. Jewell III** 2009
Minister Of Music (RIP)

"Relationships Are Like Seasons...
They Only Last So Long
Within The Trueness of Its Time."

- **Yolanda Adams** 2006
Personal Sister and Inspirational Artist

Re: Any Task or Project
"Begin With The End In Mind"

- **Michael Aaron Saunders** 2007
Personal Brother

WITTY NOTES

"If You Concern Yourself With
What People Say Bad About You...
You Will Drive Your Own Self Crazy."

- **Maulty C. Jewell III** 2008
Minister Of Music

Re: Leadership
**"Those Closest To You
Are Most Times The Hardest To Lead...**
and ***"More Than Apt"*** (more than likely)
To Be The Fastest Ones To Hurt You."

- Rev. Pharis D. Evans 2014
Pastor/Daddy

Re: Not Knowing Theory
**"Theory Is A Matter Of Labels.
Theory Will Tell You Something Shouldn't Be
Played (created) A Certain Way –
But If It Sounds Good To You... Go With It."**

- Maulty Jewell IV aka Tuff 2015
Closest Personal Brother & Music Partner

"Many People Have Degrees
But No Temperature.
Study To Show Yourself Approved
To God...Not Man."

- **Samuel R. Blakes** 2016
Personal Friend, Pastor & Artist

WITTY NOTES

"You Will Always Reap
WHAT You Sow,
But You Won't Always Reap "from"
WHERE You Sow."

- Samuel R. Blakes 2017
Personal Friend, Pastor & Artist

WITTY NOTES

"When Your Heart Is To Help,
But You Discover
Your Help Is Not Helping...
STOP!"

- Joseph E. Davis 2018
Personal Friend, Pastor & Mentor

"MUCH REAL LOVE"

The End

WITTY NOTES

ABOUT THE AUTHOR

Pharis Evans Jr. is a Writer/Producer, Music Clinician, Recording Artist, Motivational Speaker, Author and last but not least a Minister, which affords him various brand titles, and makes him a man of multifarious interests. But in all that he is and does, PEJ is ready, willing and able, to service the world: One man, with many brands of purpose, dressed for duty, and equipped to execute.

Pharis' books reveal various information to his readers by way of transparency, experience, wisdom and revelation from on high. Each and every book presents, offers, suggests, informs and enlightens... all with the intent and hope of seeing things from a wider and broader

perspective – with an intent for a gain of knowledge and hope for greater living. PEJ hopes to plant seeds in the minds, hearts and spirits of readers for them to fertilize the seed customized to shape the best scope and purpose with Life application.

- ❖ For questions in one's heart, PEJ hopes to provide answers.
- ❖ For problems in one's life, PEJ hopes to provide solutions.
- ❖ For darkness in one's sight, PEJ hopes to provide light.
- ❖ For uncertainty in one's mind, PEJ hopes to provide knowledge.

But most of all Pharis Evans Jr. strives to motivate, uplift and encourage.

WITTY NOTES

Made in the USA
Middletown, DE
19 August 2022

70950478R00146